DESIGN IDEAS FOR SMALL SPACES

Dining Rooms & Kitchens

First published in the United States of America by:
Rockport Publishers, Inc.
146 Granite Street
Rockport, Massachusetts 01966-1299
Telephone: (508) 546-9590
Fax: (508) 546-7141

ISBN 1-56496-303-9

10 9 8 7 6 5 4 3 2 1

Layout: Sara Day Graphic Design
Cover Credit: See page 41

Printed by Welpac, Singapore.

DESIGN IDEAS FOR SMALL SPACES

Dining Rooms & Kitchens

Norman Smith

ROCKPORT
PUBLISHERS

Rockport Publishers
Rockport, Massachusetts

INTRODUCTION

Small space design is about making a lot out of a little. Whether you live in an urban townhouse, a suburban apartment or a single family house, increased costs for land, construction, and materials have caused buildings to become more efficient and to accommodate more in increasingly smaller physical envelopes.

The obvious limitation of a small space is its size. That limitation can be a small overall building size, a room with little square footage, a low ceiling, a cramped building site with no views or room for additions outward, or the need to squeeze too many functions and uses in too little space.

Small kitchens and dining rooms often suffer from poor traffic patterns; in other words, the movement of people through and around the space. Also, a comfortable layout for cabinets or furniture is often difficult to achieve in a tiny kitchen or abbreviated dining area. Poor design is magnified in a small space: A room that looks cramped or cluttered, dark, unappealing, and at times even oppressive is, without a doubt, an ineffective and unsuccessful space.

A small kitchen or dining space can take many forms. It can be a tiny, galley-style kitchen, or a medium-size eating area that doubles as a home office. It might be a niche-like banquette carved from the living areas, or a studio kitchen that uses imaginative storage ideas to save valuable countertop and floor space. It might be a loft space that frees up floor area to create a dining room, or a piece of custom furniture that acts as a room divider by separating a small kitchen from the adjacent dining space and hallway.

Imaginative uses of both natural and artificial light to backlight a space, and make it appear larger than its true size, are well worth adopting in any design plan where space is tight. Cooking and eating areas combined in one space can be differentiated with complementary colors of paint or materials on the walls and ceilings. Likewise, creating or focusing attention on a view—whether outside or in the room—can visually expand an otherwise cramped area.

The purpose of this book is to explore small space design by illustrating the many individual concepts and approaches of designers and architects confronted with the problems of small spaces. The kitchens and dining rooms in these pages employ a variety of design tools or 'devices'. As you will see, while the devices appear again and again, their final effect changes according to the designer's choices, the use of the space, and the many other factors that go into a finished design.

Whether you are a homeowner planning your own remodeling project, or a professional designer, you should view a small kitchen or dining room as an opportunity rather than a lost cause. While it may seem daunting at first, no small space is beyond hope or is impossible to improve: Any room or space can be designed or remodeled to appear larger and more attractive.

DESIGN, AESTHETICS, AND STYLE

Photographer: Walter Smalling

A well-built design project must be detailed and constructed properly.

Creating a good design plan is a lot like sculpting a figure or painting a picture. Then, that thought is translated from the mind to reality in the same way that a sculptor begins with a block of stone or a painter moves to the canvas. Finally, the initial concept is refined using the tools of each person's trade. For a sculptor, a hammer and chisels bring the idea to light, while for the painter, brushes and pigments suffice. For the designer, the essential concept is first tempered by the need to satisfy three basic qualities. Paraphrasing an ancient architectural theorist, all designs must be well-built and useable while incorporating a strong measure of delight.

Each of these basics is related to all the others so that when artfully conceived, the whole is a wonderful sum of these parts. The loss of any one of these qualities or an imbalance among them can make a design lackluster and unusable.

The design starts with an essential concept much like a thought or a wish. In small space designs, this care is manifested by the artful detailing of portions of the design and by the efficient, imaginative, and conscientious use of materials. Sensitivity to the interior and exterior environment is an important part of building. Simultaneously, the manipulation of a room's proportions must come into play for both aesthetic effect and ease in construction. The use of symmetry or, alternately, asymmetry in the structural layout affects the cost of a design and its feeling of openness.

Along with the sense of construction, the design must be useable and must satisfy basic functional requirements. In a small space, this can be as simple as increasing light and air and as complicated as integrating multiple uses in a tightly defined room. Again, a designer's sense of appropriate proportions must come into play to help shape the space effectively.

Just as proportions affect the feel of a room, the use of one or more focal points can create the appearance of spaciousness or alternately that of a cozy and enclosed retreat within the space. Spatial and depth perception can be manipulated to visually transform a small space. For instance, a wall can be angled to counteract the natural shortening of perspective, making a room seem larger or longer, while still accommodating required traffic patterns through the space. The use of symmetry to balance competing elements can lend an air of quiet repose to a small room while providing for an efficient use of the space. In a different situation, an asymmetrical layout might help counter unequal uses and impart a feeling of dynamic excitement to an otherwise plain room. Continuity and discontinuity are also often associated with small space design. Making a surface discontinuous reinforces a sense of separation; on the other hand, a continuous patch of unbroken floor can be used to tie together several adjacent small spaces so that each appears a part of the others.

Delight is the third part of the essential triumvirate but it is of a piece with all the rest. Delight is often confused with aesthetics and style. However, aesthetics is really just the pursuit and appreciation of beauty in its many forms. Various styles are, and have become over time, the accepted manifestation of a current standard of beauty. However, the phrase 'aesthetics and style' is often used as though they have a life of their own and are merely a window dressing that can be applied to any room, almost like throwing on a change of clothes. Nothing could be further from the truth.

From a designer's standpoint the overall atmosphere of a space, or its aesthetic, is not simply a question of overlaying a style. Rather, it is dictated by the interaction of all three essential elements. These requirements are then filtered through the designer's mind and mixed with the variables of budget and other requirements to produce a final aesthetic that is appropriate for each particular situation.

Finally, the design is further refined and made concrete with the tools or devices of the designers trade to produce a final product. These devices are part and parcel of every small space design and, in different ways, will always reflect the three essential qualities and their related concepts.

Photographer: Walter Smalling

While it is possible to redo rooms in different period styles to pleasurable effect, the best small space designs don't start with a style but rather with the designer's and owner's fundamental thoughts and needs.

BASIC CONCEPTS OF SMALL SPACE DESIGN

A design is shaped by the designer's knowledge of how these qualities are first realized. This occurs through the use of the designer's equivalent of canvas or stone, using several basic design concepts including:

SYMMETRY/ASYMMETRY refers to a plan configuration or to the three-dimensional treatment of surfaces and planes within a space. In an effort to resolve fundamental building and design problems, designers have begun experimenting with more extreme forms of asymmetry. It is frequently used in small space design for exactly this reason.

PROPORTION is essentially the relationship of parts to the whole both in two dimensions and in three. Certain proportional relationships are pleasing to the mind and eye while others can create a disharmonious appearance.

FOCUS/FOCAL POINTS can be one of the basic building blocks of any small space design. Creating a main focal point in a small space can minimize other unattractive but necessary intrusions in the space. A focal point can be many things; a painting on a wall, the wall itself, a superb cabinet, a view outside, or any number of other items.

SPATIAL/DEPTH PERCEPTION relates to the overall appearance of a space. A skillful designer can deliberately manipulate elements of the design to make the room feel larger or smaller, shorter or taller, narrower or wider, depending on the situation.

CONTINUITY/DISCONTINUITY applies to the nature of a surface or to the layout of a plan. Continuity usually melds or ties together disparate elements; discontinuity heightens differences to create an appealing tension.

As a design progresses, these qualities and concepts are combined in any number of ways to refine the initial thought.

HOW TO USE THIS BOOK

For the purposes of this book, eight different devices have been chosen to help explain the different approaches of the various small space designs and their respective designers.

While no design will employ every possible device and some will certainly employ more than just a few, it's still possible to look at small space design as a compendium of these tools and to imagine how these devices might be applied to other designs, including your own.

Plan Organization

Basic plan devices include:

a. A layout of one or more spaces that incorporates circulation or alternately, that reconfigures a space to remove circulation in order to make the space more useable.

b. An orientation of a room or space to the outdoors to make the interior space feel larger. Aligning openings or using similar or sympathetic materials can help blend an interior space with an exterior space such as a patio or enclosed courtyard.

c. A physical connection or adjacency that opens up one or more areas to another.

Structure

Although structure may seem like just the utilitarian bones that help hold up roofs and floors, when expertly revealed and arranged, the structure defines space and suggests connections in very subtle ways.

Many designers will use structural necessities, such as bearing posts and beams, to create a delicate layering of line and shadow within a small space. This overlay can help define specific areas without the need for full-height walls, while still producing an overall feeling of openness.

Surfaces

Modulation of wall, ceiling, and floor surfaces can produce rich and varied textures that enliven even the smallest room. Surface variations can also be employed to affect how light fills the room. For instance, a mottled or highly textured surface diffuses light; while a polished or lacquered plane reflects it. Surface treatments range from basic wallpaper and paint to such esoteric materials as stainless steel, custom paint finishes, and special woods.

Color

Like surfaces, use of color can often make or break a design. In a small space, color can be used to highlight or de-emphasize a particular surface or object. Well chosen colors can be used to tie several small rooms together, or alternately, to subtly differentiate them. Color can be used to make surfaces recede or to draw them closer to the eye. Natural and artificial lighting greatly contributes to the perceived size of a room. Depending on the intention, a murky chiaroscuro or a bright, almost stark appearance can be used to open up a space or create a focus within a room.

Natural light can be introduced unaltered via windows and skylights or it can be filtered and modified through deep recesses, window treatments or other means.

Lighting fixtures are currently available in an almost bewildering array of types and designs. Like natural light, artificial lighting can be used indirectly to merely suggest a warm glow or at the other extreme, the lighting fixture itself can be made a bright and dazzling centerpiece to the room.

Lighting

Attention to details such as trim, connections, and hardware is important in all designs, but in a small space the importance of detail cannot be overlooked. Well-crafted details can suggest a richness that belies a small project budget. At the same time, details can introduce a perceptual scale change that camouflages the true dimensions of a small space.

Trim and Detail

Connecting inside and outside spaces is a time-honored device that is particularly appropriate to small space design. By sharing or borrowing space from the outside, almost any room can be made to feel larger and more gracious. The connection may be as simple as a lushly planted garden casually placed outside a pair of glass doors or as complicated as the rigorous use of similar or sympathetic materials that continue from indoors to the outside.

Inside and Outside

Designers often employ built-in and carefully selected pieces of furniture to maintain and reinforce their aesthetic intent. In a small space, this aesthetic control is still important but furniture design and placement can, quite simply, save space—or at least use the space more efficiently. Striking material palettes in furniture can also be used to complement the background surfaces.

Furniture

Not all of these design devices are appropriate for every project; using every device in a small project would be like ordering every item from an a la carte menu; the meal would simply be too large, too rich, and lacking the focus of a single well executed entree. In much the same way, most designers go through an editing process to try to achieve a simplicity and clarity of design. As you will see, each project illustrated in this book utilizes one or more of these design devices to make a small space useable and, at the same time, a delight to use.

Kitchens

T he increase in two or more career households—coupled with small space requirements—makes the kitchen the new center of the house for both cooking and time spent together.

Fortunately, the center need not be large, as the projects that follow will illustrate. Creating eat-in kitchens is good space utilization that preserves open vistas both inside and out. Windows and doors that borrow space from the outside can lend a much needed expansiveness to compact kitchens. Calculated asymmetry can also be used to help distinguish individual areas within the larger whole.

Simply making the kitchen work on a functional level is not enough. In some projects, the kitchen and dining areas have an ongoing conversation through the use of compatible or contrasting materials that differentiate but do not disguise one space from the other. Thoughtful use of materials on cabinetry and surfaces can reinforce different cooking and eating areas within the combined whole, or can help exaggerate the feel of an otherwise minimally dimensioned separate space. In other projects, the kitchen itself is the focus, and is made to feel larger and more inviting through the use of various materials and surfaces that add a glint of light or an airy feeling.

SMALL KITCHENS

Photographer: Cindy Linkins

 A finely detailed pot rack takes the place of wall cabinets to maintain the view outdoors.

 A large proportion of glass to wall makes the pavilion appear to float and helps disguise its attachment to the house.

SUBURBAN KITCHEN ADDITION

This addition to a non-descript suburban house takes advantage of beautiful backyard views by planting a classically inspired, pavilion-like structure at the edge of an existing slope. Inside, the kitchen expands out to the landscape through a series of windows. At the same time, low cabinetry and elegant but minimal detailing emphasize the view without getting in the way.

TOWNHOUSE KITCHEN RENOVATION

In this townhouse, the small kitchen and dining spaces are left open to one another while both also open to an adjacent family room addition. Custom cabinetry and built-ins, along with brightly colored structural steel, help to define individual work and sitting areas within the larger space.

 The kitchen and dining room share space, but a tall back-splash at the countertop hides food preparation and clean-up.

 Semi-gloss paint on the surfaces of exposed kitchen cabinets and on the fireplace surround gives normal scale objects the appearance of monolithic mass with low-key detailing.

 Through the family room, the kitchen opens onto a patio with a second-story, metal-roofed deck as a backdrop.

Photographer: Julia Heine

Photographer: Tim Street-Porter

OPEN PLAN STUDIO KITCHEN

Treating a necessary staircase as a decorative object spilling into the space adds a note of humor and also helps to define different areas.

The banquette disguises the kitchen's small size and is also a smooth transitional element from entry area to kitchen work space.

This plan incorporates studio, sleeping, and kitchen space in one small building. A series of asymmetrical and sinuous curves reveals the interior in stages as it winds around the kitchen. A banquette seating area matches up with the stair.

Open-Ceiling Kitchen

B oth the functional and spatial centerpiece of the house, this kitchen illustrates how a small space gains stature as it expands up to the skylight roof of the house and the adjacent stair.

 At a certain vantage point, the exploded ceiling is only partially revealed but still lets in plenty of natural light.

 The wood surfaces of the kitchen walls continue into the open stairway above, unifying the space and drawing the eye upward.

Photographer: © Walter Smalling Jr.

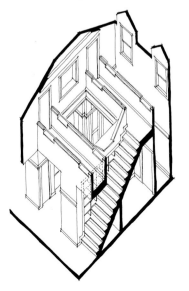

17

Photographer: Julia Heine

Mottled green walls complement the light, sandy color and grain of the ash paneling, adding texture without chopping up the space visually.

Openings in the paneled wall make a narrow kitchen seem wider.

Shared wall materials used in other adjacent rooms unify the kitchen with the rest of the house.

GALLERY KITCHEN RENOVATION

A renovation of kitchen and adjacent dining and living areas, this project uses a subtle, ash-veneer plywood on cabinets, and as wall paneling, to link the spaces visually. The paneling camouflages storage doors along the hallway and continues out to form cabinetry and paneling in the adjacent rooms.

GALLEY KITCHEN

A directional floor pattern leading to a set of windows helps to visually expand the narrow kitchen in a small suburban home.

Paint and wood trim on the ceiling act as a skylight and create a counterpoint to the lighting pattern and pattern on the floor.

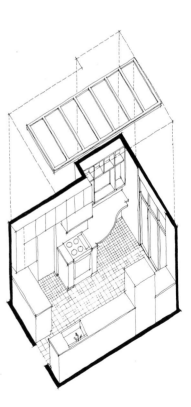

REMODELED MODERN KITCHEN

This remodeled kitchen did not involve a huge addition or an increase in square footage. Instead, circulation was re-routed, windows and skylights were added, and a restrained variety of materials were used to provide changes in wall surface and in reflectivity.

Combining maple veneer wall cabinets and paneling with warm granite countertops creates a pleasing counterpoint of cold and warm surfaces in the same space.

A custom designed light fixture serves as a focal point above the sink and balances the daylight from skylights.

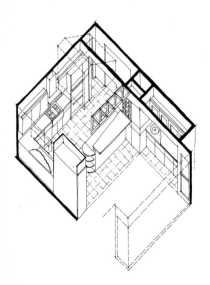

Photographer: M. Kibbey

 At the sink's broken granite backsplash and barsink top, the granite trim is treated as a material to be shaped and detailed rather than simply applied.

High windows allow direct sunlight in during certain parts of the day, keeping the small space light. A bay glazed with sandblasted glass balances the clear glass above and offers privacy from the neighboring house.

 Standard laminate cabinets are trimmed with chrome cap screws to provide a secondary level of trim on the cabinet faces.

Photographer: Norman Smith

SHALLOW LOT KITCHEN ADDITION

This 90 square foot kitchen addition is fitted into a shallow in-town lot and creates space for a functional kitchen and small attached breakfast bay. Outside, a sharply gabled copper-clad roof creates a strong visual image for the tiny addition, while providing a shaded overhang for the clerestory windows.

Photographer: Norman Smith

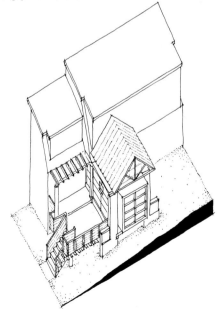

 A compact kitchen unit by Siematic, tucked to the side of a family or living area, demonstrates the space-saving possibilities of this type of layout.

 Slick, finished surfaces define the kitchen as a separate area without the use of walls.

SPACE-SAVING KITCHEN

Photographer: *Paul Warchol*

WAREHOUSE STUDIO KITCHEN

A combination studio/living space in a gutted warehouse provides a two-story work area with kitchen/dining areas at the rear of the space.

 The textured surface of glass panels attached to exposed wood studs provides a subtle division between the kitchen and adjacent bathroom.

 Maple and stainless steel are combined to form an idiosyncratic vision of the kitchen sink.

RENTAL UNIT KITCHEN REHAB

G iven a tight budget and only about 700 square feet in this rental unit, the architects artfully manipulated basic colors and surfaces to suggest textural richness and spaciousness.

 A translucent wall surface facing into the hallway screens the kitchen area while hinting at spaces beyond.

 Vibrant recessed ceiling cut-outs contrast with the otherwise monochromatic color scheme and create focal points of color in different areas.

 Minimal track lighting in conjunction with skylights and the soft diffused light of the kitchen wall makes for a pleasing variety of lighting effects.

Photographer: Kiss Cathcart Anders

Photographer: Julia Heine

BUNGALOW KITCHEN

 The use of 2 over 2 windows with transoms above allows light to penetrate deeply into the small kitchen work space.

 The decorative tile work and painted wood surfaces blend the new addition with the older, mail-order style, wood house.

Dining Rooms

Even if all parts of an abode are equal, the kitchen and dining areas are the most equal. The trend in small space design is toward separate but open dining areas that share space with the kitchen. By paying careful attention to surface treatments, colors, and lighting, you can give visual expansiveness and stature to a small dining space. Additions of custom cabinetry, built-ins, or brightly colored structural materials, can define individual work and sitting areas within a larger space. Also, matching wood surfaces, veneer on cabinets, or wall paneling from the kitchen to the dining alcove will unify the space and draw the eye upward.

In open-plan designs, pay attention to making adjoining rooms complementary: Shared wall materials or varying shades of a single color will visually link the dining room with the other spaces. Surface textures, rather than color, can also be used to add interest and to create contrast without appearing cut-up.

Built-in seating, such as a banquette that follows the plane of a wall, will maximize a small floor area and emphasize the shape of the dining room or alcove. If the space is narrow, adding recessed wall openings will create focal points and make the room seem wider.

Lighting can also be used to create focal points and the illusion of more space: spot lighting the table surface, or using deeply recessed, vertical windows to bring in the sun, will create a provocative play of light and shadow without taking up floor space.

SMALL DINING ROOMS

LOFT DINING ROOM

This gallery/entertainment design juxtaposes sophisticated furniture and the primitive appearance of the walls and structure to create a contradictory but appealing atmosphere in a tight space.

 A table area is defined by vertical, exposed wood posts and the exposed wood structure of the ceiling above.

 Overhead task-lighting reinforces the functional divisions within this small dining room.

· Photographer: Peter Olson

32

Photographer: Cindy Linkins

MINIMALIST DINING AREA

 A restrained palette of pastel and mid-value colors helps mark the end of the kitchen and the beginning of this small eating area.

 Architect-designed seating is minimally detailed to de-emphasize the projection into the adjacent living space.

 A single, asymmetrically located column also helps to define the corner without adding visual clutter.

SUSPENDED CEILING DINING ROOM

 A narrow dining area is given definition and a sense of grandeur with the manipulation of a curved ceiling plane. The plane does not touch the walls and seems to float above the table, defining the space without constricting it visually.

 A series of light colors step down in value through the play of light and shadow, visually enlarging this dining room.

Photographer: Norman McGrath

Photographer: *Erik Kvalsvik*

LOFT DINING ALCOVE

 This dining space is an adjunct to a larger, open area which also accommodates the bedroom. The area is set off by a lowered ceiling height and elegantly detailed metal ladders.

 Metal ceiling panels and sliding doors that open to the kitchen are strong focal points within the space and help to tie the kitchen and dining areas together.

 A medium yellow hue on the end walls contrasts with the steel and balances the interior composition.

CONDOMINIUM DINING ROOM

 Rather than chopping up the space with walls, the dining area in this open plan condominium is set off by ceiling height changes and dropped beams.

 Use of a deep, saturated teal green and warm, charcoal grey on adjacent walls brings added depth to the small space.

 A custom designed table of ebonized mahogany, cherry, and aluminum provides a sharp visual contrast to the opaque wall surfaces.

Photographer: Norman Smith

CONVERTIBLE DINING AREA

 Building a pull-out table into base cabinets allows the table to be stored away when not in use.

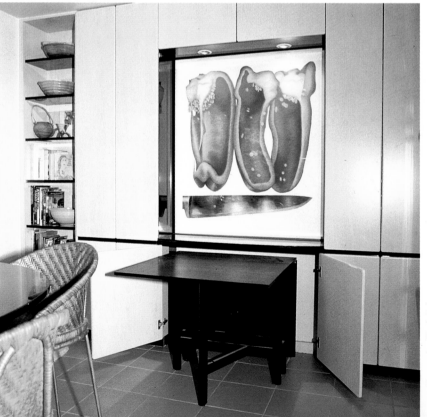

Photographer: Woody Cady

Photographer: Undine Prohl

MODERN PLAN
URBAN KITCHEN

Metal posts demarcate family, dining, and kitchen areas while allowing all three areas to be considered one space.

A dishwasher encased in finished plywood takes back wasted space and acts as a base for the "unsupported" kitchen sink top.

Two-Story Dining Room

A small, lake-side house is divided into three distinct volumes for living spaces, bedrooms, and bathrooms, respectively. The living and dining areas are accommodated in a diminutive two-story volume, each borrowing space and light from the other.

A loft-like space, accessible by ladder, adds space and forms the ceiling of the dining area.

Photographer: Gregory Murphey

Photographer: Richard Mandelkorn

Conservatory Dining Room

A delicately framed and detailed atrium defines views outward and pulls a small urban garden into the house.

Continuing the glazing onto the ceiling floods the space with light, and makes the boundaries of the structure seem to disappear.

STUDIO DINING ROOM ADDITION

 Remodeling an existing stair opens up the old dining room to views through a new studio addition. Although the dining room's compact size remains untouched, it seems larger now that it is part of a more gracious assembly of interlocking spaces.

 The insertion of various shelving units and matching rails helps tie together the trim elements to create an almost monumental overlook.

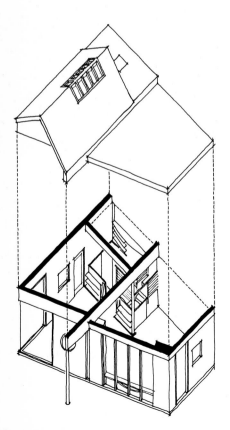

Photographer: Shorieh Talaat Design Associates

Photographer: Undine Pröhl

INDOOR/OUTDOOR DINING ROOM

 One simple gesture, the use of a finely but simply detailed window that allows the table top to literally extend outside, completely transforms the orientation of this small eating area.

 The massively proportioned table becomes a sculptural element within the space and is subtly complemented by the restrained color and texture of the stone floor.

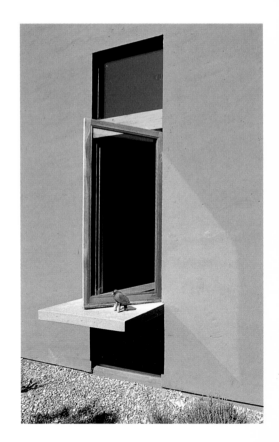

DIRECTORY OF ARCHITECTS

DIRECTORY OF CONTRACTORS

DIRECTORY OF PHOTOGRAPHERS

Kiss Cathcart Anders
150 Nassau Street
Suite 2300
New York, NY 10038

Woody Cady
Woody Cady Photography
4512-A Avondale Street
Bethesda, MD 20814

Julia Heine
310 1/2 A Street NE
Washington, DC 20002

Mussy Kibbey
3036 Hillegass Avenue
Berkeley, CA 94705

Erik Kvalsvik
106 West University Parkway
Baltimore, MD 21210

Cindy Linkins
Shorieh Talaat Design
Associates
15715 Kruhm Road
Burtonsville, MD 20866

Richard Mandelkorn
65 Beaver Pond Road
Lincoln, MA 01773
Norman McGrath
164 West 79th Street
New York, NY 10024

Gregory Murphey
Rural Route #2
Box 191
Trafalgar, IN 46181

Peter Olson
211 North 13th Street
Philadelphia, PA 19107-1624

Undine Pröhl
1930 Ocean Avenue #302
Santa Monica, CA 90405

SieMatic Corporation
886 Town Center Drive
Langhorne, PA 19047

Walter Smalling
1541 Eighth Street NW
Washington, DC 20001

Norman Smith
3800 Military Road NW
Washington, DC 20015

Tim Street-Porter
2074 Watsonia Terrace
Los Angeles, CA 90068

Shorieh Talaat Design
Associates
15715 Kruhm Road
Burtonsville, MD 20866

Paul Warchol
133 Mulberry Street
New York, NY 10013